# TWISTERS
## and Other Wind Storms

# *Contents*

# Wind Storms

*Written by Tracey Reeder*
*Illustrated by Geoffrey Cox*

Wind storms are very scary!
Wind storms can smash up buildings
and push over trees. Wind storms
over the sea can make very big waves
that can flood the land.

Wind storms happen
when hot and cold air meet.

These wind storms are
- tornadoes or twisters
- hurricanes or tropical cyclones
  or typhoons
- cyclones

All of these storms have winds
that go round in a circle.

Wind is air going from one place to another.

# Tornadoes or Twisters

Tornadoes are also called twisters.

Tornadoes are the most dangerous wind storms because they have the fastest winds.

Tornadoes begin in dark clouds.
A funnel cloud comes out of the dark cloud and points down to the ground.
The wind blows round in a circle and gets faster and faster.
If the funnel reaches the ground, it can suck up and smash anything in its path!

What are waterspouts? Waterspouts are tornadoes over the sea.

Tornadoes have winds
that can be more than 200 mph (322 kph)!
The very biggest tornadoes
are only about 1½ miles (2.4 km) across.

Warm air

Cold air

Find out what
mph and kph
mean.

# Hurricanes

Hurricanes are also called tropical cyclones
or typhoons.

Hurricanes can be very big.
They can be up to 200–300 miles (322–483 km) wide.
These winds go round in a circle like tornado winds.
The middle of a hurricane is called the eye.
The wind doesn't blow in the eye of a hurricane.

Hurricanes start over the sea. They bring big waves,
heavy rain, and fast winds to the land.

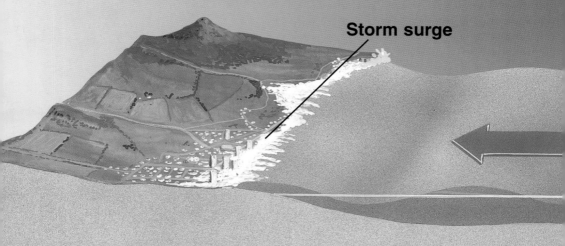

**Storm surge**

A storm surge is when a hurricane
blows the sea at the land.

The word *hurricane* comes from the Carib-Indian word for *big wind*. Near China and the West Indies, people call hurricanes typhoons. The word *typhoon* comes from the Chinese word meaning *great wind*.

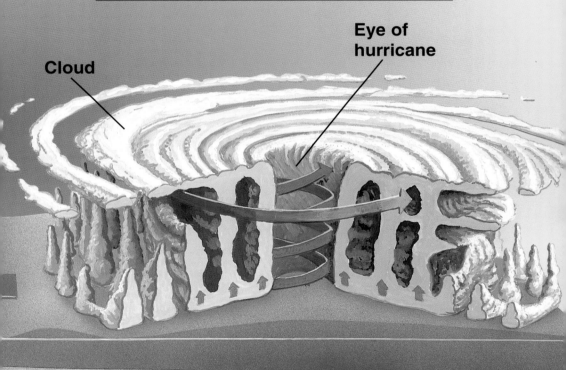

**Cloud**

**Eye of hurricane**

The winds in a hurricane can move very fast. Hurricanes have winds that are 73 mph (117.5 kph) or faster.

# Cyclones

A cyclone can cover an area as big as
one-third of the United States!

A cyclone starts when warm air meets cold air.
The line where the two winds meet is called a front.
When the warm air and cold air meet, the warm air
moves up on top of the cold air.
As it moves up, the warm air gets cooler
and forms clouds.
The wind starts to blow in a circle into the middle
of the storm. The air pressure starts to fall.
The low pressure area is called a cyclone.

Cyclones are wet windy storms.

Stop and think.
Do you know
the difference
between a tornado,
a hurricane, and a
cyclone?

The word *cyclone* comes from the Greek word
meaning *wheel* or *coil*. The winds go round
in a circle like the coil of a snake.

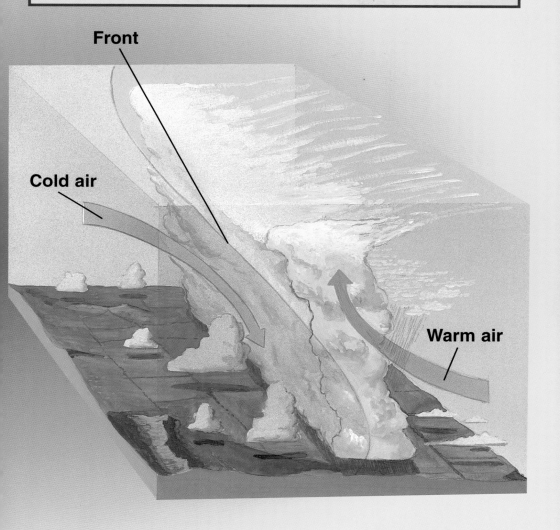

Front

Cold air

Warm air

Cyclones have winds
that are 39–72 mph (63–116 kph).

# Hurricane Andrew

Do you know how hurricanes get their names? Where can you find out?

*Written by Paul Reeder*

In August 1992, a big hurricane
hit the Bahamas, Florida, and Louisiana.
The hurricane was called Andrew.
The winds in the hurricane
blew from 145 to nearly 200 miles per hour
(233–322 kph).

Hurricane Andrew started on August 13.
The hurricane started as thunderstorms
over western Africa.
The storm blew out over the Atlantic Ocean.
By Monday, August 17,
the storm had turned into a tropical storm.
The winds were going round in a circle.

By Saturday, August 22,
the winds were blowing
as fast as 74 miles per hour (119 kph).
The storm was now a hurricane!
By Sunday, August 23,
the winds were 150 miles per hour (241 kph)!

Florida

**This is Hurricane Andrew over the Gulf of Mexico.
Andrew has already passed over Florida.**

No one knows just how fast the winds blew
when the storm was full on,
because the hurricane stopped
the measuring equipment working.

Hurricane Andrew caused a lot of damage.

It ripped 80,000 houses apart
and 50,000 houses had only parts left standing.
It damaged big buildings, too.

Hurricane Andrew blew away thousands of cars.
It ripped out thousands and thousands of trees.
It blew boats up onto the land
and ripped out power poles and traffic lights.
It ripped out water pipes and blew away road signs.

Lots of people were left with nowhere to live.
Lots of people lost everything they owned.

Make a list
of all the words
that could describe
how the people
felt.

After the storm there were bits of wood and tin, pipes and wires, and furniture and clothes all over the ground.

There was no food, no water, and no power.

The National Guard was called to help.
Some of the National Guard showed people
where it was safe to drive.
Some cleaned up the mess.
Some helped cook food and hand out water.
Some looked for lost people.
Some looked after shops and houses
to stop people stealing things.

More helpers came from all over the United States.
The cleaning up started.

# The Long Night

**Written by Tracey Reeder**
**Illustrated by Rick Youmans**

Hi, my name is Manuel.

I live in a mobile home in Florida.

Our home is in a park
with lots of other mobile homes.
We grow flowers outside our home,
and sometimes we sit out in the sun.
My brother Paulo
says our home is very pretty.
Well, it was pretty
before the tornado!

When I went to bed that night
everything was fine.
Then Dad woke us up!
I could hear the wind blowing.

Dad said, "Get up! Quick!
There's a tornado warning!"

Dad said he had just seen the news
on television.
A tornado was coming!
Dad said the weather people
can only tell you about 15 or 20 minutes
before the tornado hits.

"Quick," said Dad, "get under the table."

My brother grabbed my hand.
My mother had our baby sister
and the dog.
We all got under the table.

Dad opened the door
and shouted to the other families,
"Tornado! Tornado!
A tornado is coming!
Get somewhere safe!"

Then Dad got under the table
with us.

Do you think
the safest place
to go in a tornado
is under a table?

The wind was very strong now.
I could hear people shouting.
Then the wind seemed to stop.
I thought the tornado was over.
I tried to get out from under the table,
but Dad held onto me.

"No," he said, "just wait.
That's not the end of it."

Then the wind started again.
The room began to shake.
I could hear the windows smashing.
Glass was flying all around inside.
Then the door blew in.
There was a ripping sound all around us.
The wind was everywhere!
The table we were under began to shake,
and then it was gone!
I put my hands over my face
and stayed down.
Just as I thought
we would all get sucked into the storm,
the wind died down.

We all got up.

Paulo said there was glass and wood
and tin all over the place.
All the mobile homes were smashed up.
He said most of the trees were gone.
The only tree still standing
had a car in it!

My mother and father were very upset.
They were looking at
what was left of our home.
They said it wasn't pretty now.
Our home didn't have a roof,
or windows, or doors.
And it had a truck
in what had been our bedroom!
Our flowers were gone.
Our clothes and furniture
were all over the place.
What a mess!

Dad hugged us all.
He said we were very lucky.
We still had each other.
Our family wasn't hurt.

How can
you tell from
the story that
Manuel can't
see?

# El Niño

*Written by Paul Reeder*

The fishermen of Peru gave the name El Niño
to a warm sea current that seemed to come
at Christmas in some years.

When El Niño came, the weather changed, too.

## El Niño Facts

El Niño begins when the sea
in the eastern Pacific Ocean gets warm
and the air pressure is low.
This makes the winds change the way they blow.
The winds blow from west to east.
The winds blow along the top of the ocean,
and the warm sea is pushed
to the coasts of North and South America.
Rainfall follows the warm water.
The hot air over the oceans
also brings thunderstorms.

The El Niño in 1997–1998
changed the weather in many countries:

- California had lots of storms.
- Peru and Equador had heavy rains and floods.
- Parts of New Zealand, Australia,
  Papua New Guinea, Indonesia, Malaysia,
  and Asia didn't have any rain.

# From Canterbury, New Zealand

My name is John Greene.
I'm a sheep farmer in New Zealand.
El Niño hasn't been good for us!

We haven't had any rain for six months.
All the water for our home comes from the rain.
It runs off the roof and goes into big tanks.
We have to watch how much water we use
so we don't run out.

We have five creeks on the farm,
but they have all dried up.
The grass turned brown and died,
so the sheep are hungry,
and they need water to drink.
All the farms around us are the same.
The New Zealand Army is helping all the farmers
by bringing in tankers full of water.
We are feeding the sheep hay to keep them alive,
but their wool won't be very good this year.

We didn't think El Niño would last so long.
We all hope El Niño will go away soon!

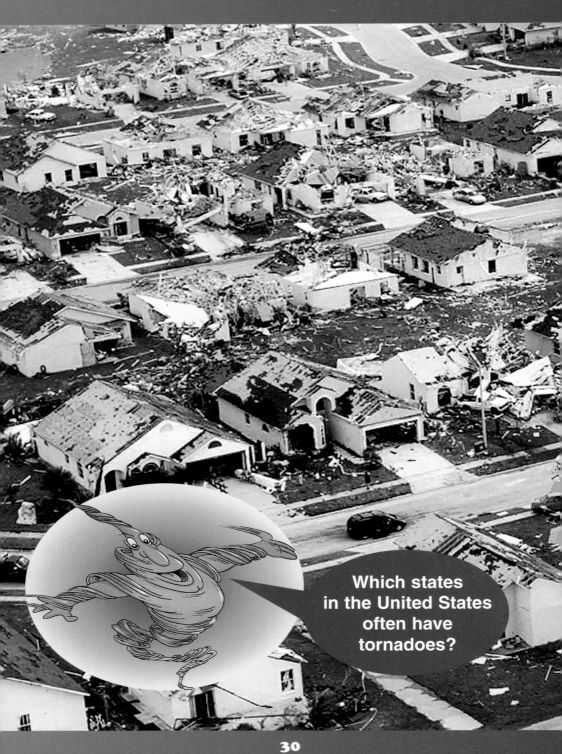

# *From Seminole County, Florida*

My name is Louisa Brown.
I live in Seminole County, Florida.

El Niño has not been good for me!
El Niño brought a lot of tornadoes to Florida,
and one tornado hit the place where I live.

The roof was ripped off my house,
and everything I own was blown away.
But the worst part was that my little boy
was sucked out of his bed by the tornado!
When the wind started to blow, I ran to his room.
The roof was coming off the house as I ran.
When I got there, my son and his bed were gone!
I didn't think I would ever see him alive again.
I tried to get outside to find him,
but the wind was too strong!
When the wind stopped, my friend came running over.
She had my son in her arms!

He was safe!

I hope this is the last time El Niño comes!

# Index